YAR

THE STRAIGHTFORWARD CV

HOWARD ROGERS

Straightforward Publishing Limited
38 Cromwell Road, London E17 9JN

© Straightforward Publishing
First Edition 1996

British Library Cataloguing in Publication data. A catalogue record for this book is available from the British Library.

ISBN: 1 8999224 40 X

Printed in Great Britain by BPC Wheatons Ltd, Exeter
Cover design by Straightforward Graphics.

CONTENTS

INTRODUCTION

The objective of this book is to demonstrate the most effective way of formulating the ideal CV.

The way we present ourselves to a prospective employer is very important and can mean the difference between getting a job we want and failing. Presenting ourselves begins with the CV which is the first contact that an employer will have with us. Although many people know the basics of putting a CV together, there is a big difference between those who have studied the technique and those who have not.

Many applicants undersell themselves right at the outset with a poorly laid out CV which contains too little information. The purpose of this book is to enable those who read it to ensure that the best possible CV is formulated, a CV which shows the applicant in the best light and which provides a stepping stone to the all important interview.

Your CV won't actually get you a job. This happens at the interview stage. It will, however, get you through the door and put you in the race. Because your CV is so important it is obvious that it should be as neat as possible, presented on good quality paper and accurate in all respects. Remember that your CV is being looked at cold by someone who has never met you and therefore first impressions count for everything.

The book assumes that you will be applying for jobs within the United Kingdom. If this is not the case, you must research the company even more thoroughly and fall in with local customs. For example, in some countries of the world, it is customary to tell the employer in what high esteem you hold them and that you want this particular job more than any other job. This approach would not be acceptable in the UK..

The approach this book takes is to build up an effective CV as it progresses and also offers advice to the job hunter in such areas as writing the ideal covering letter and also how to construct particular types of CVs depending on your circumstances. Application forms are also dealt with.

Throughout this book the masculine gender has been used for ease. However, obviously the information is for male and female alike.

Good luck in your job hunting!

1

THE JOB ADVERTISEMENT

Understanding the advertisement

Understanding the job advertisement is the key to designing an effective Curriculum Vitae. Your CV needs to be formulated with that specific job in mind and it is of fundamental importance that you are able to interpret and analyse the advertisement and make correct deductions. If you do not, then your CV will miss the point and you may not progress to the next stage.

How the job is described

All advertisements will tell the reader of the name, location and business of the company. These will be put across in a positive way. Next will come the description.

Take time to think about how the job is described. This will enable you to get a real idea of what the company is after. Look to see whether you will be working alone or in a team. This is very important, particularly when emphasising skills and experience on your CV.

The company will describe what they do, what they require, then go on to outline qualifications and experience required. Obviously, this is one of the most important areas of the advertisement and should be read with care and clearly understood. In some cases, qualifications and experience required will be clearly stated. However, in other cases they won't and it will be up to you to infer these from the advert, based on your knowledge of the job.

Salary

Although, as described above, the salary attached to a job can be misleading, in many cases, the actual salary to be offered is not quoted. Statements such as "attractive salary package" or "salary commensurate with age and experience" are employed. The rule here is that if a salary is very attractive it will be quoted. Look at what is said about the salary. The word "circa" may mean around but quite often read by potential applicants as a minimum.

Many advertisements, particularly for posts in the public sector, give salary ranges. This shows interested applicants what their potential would be as well as the starting salary. Most organisations will negotiate the starting salary after they have made a decision to employ someone.

Company description and philosophy

Look at what the company has to say for itself. This usually tells you how it wants to perceive itself rather than how others see it. The company may state that it is expanding, or might give that impression by advertising for a number of positions. You might get an idea of the possible promotion prospects from the advertisement. Be wary if there is a lack of company description. This does not always mean that there is a problem, the company may be huge and well known, therefore an in depth description is not necessary. However, there may well be a flip side and the company may have something to hide, such as concealing recruitment information from other staff.

On company philosophy, look for equal opportunities statements etc. These vary enormously, with the public sector generally leading the way. You need to consider how important the existence of an equal opportunities statement is for you.

Media used to advertise position

The medium used to advertise the post can tell you a lot. If an advertisement is in a national paper then it usually means that the employer has decided that they will spend more money in order to cast their net wider, i.e., nationally instead of locally.

Some companies use agencies. This means that they have chosen to have the screening done by another party. In this case, it will be your job to convince the agency that they should put you up to the company.

Sometimes, the agency carries out initial interviews and only submits the short list to their client. You may want to consider making your application more general if the agency handles many jobs in the industry in which you work.

Think about the reasons why the organisations use agencies. Do they want specialists for whom that agency is known? Do they not have much expertise in that area themselves? This can be true when companies are seeking personnel at the top of a department, where there is nobody above with the kind of knowledge required to recruit that person.

Good advertisements are not only the right size but are also the right shape too. They have usually been professionally designed to attract the reader to the text, demonstrating careful planning and thought. Not all organisations can afford this approach. Look for simple indicators too, i.e., is the advertisement boxed? Lineage advertisements in local papers may tell you that the company is small and unsophisticated in terms of recruitment. Look at how accurately the job is described

- beware of those sounding too good to be true, few jobs live up to this.

The above are key things to look out for when reading a job advertisement. Remember, read the advertisement carefully, concentrate on each aspect building up a picture as you go. If you are in any doubt, contact the company advertising the job and request further information.

Now read the **KEY POINTS** from Chapter One.

KEY POINTS FROM CHAPTER ONE

UNDERSTANDING THE ADVERTISEMENT

- Pay careful attention to the job description in the advertisement. This will enable you to get a clear idea of what the company wants

- Most organisations will negotiate the starting salary after they have made a decision to employ someone

- Read the company description carefully and try to determine the company philosophy

- The medium used by the organisation to advertise the post will tell you a lot about the organisation

- If the company uses an agency, you may want to structure your CV a little differently

Now turn to Chapter Two.

2

DESIGNING THE IDEAL CV

Having examined and analysed the job advertised, you should now be in a position to begin constructing your CV.

Fundamental requirements of a CV

The letters "CV" stand for Curriculum Vitae, which derives from Latin. Translated, this means "the way your life has run". Correspondingly, the CV is a personal statement which demonstrates to the employer the way your life has run. The CV will usually start from your early education and progress through to higher education and chronicle your employment. It will also chronicle your personal interests. The end product should present a well rounded picture of yourself.

A CV serves several basic requirements. Firstly, it highlights your potential value to an employer. It also provides a framework within which an interview can be guided and acts as a record of the interview, or its substance.

Many people suffer mental blocks when required to formulate a CV. It can be hard work. Time and effort plus creativity are key components of the task.

The most important point to remember at the outset is that the CV should be concise and easy to read. All of the relevant and most important facts should be present.

The layout of the ideal CV

Before any information has been entered onto the CV, consideration needs to be given to the layout. By layout, I mean the actual design of the visual presentation. Remember that a better impression will be made if the person reading the CV feels comfortable with what they are reading. Effective visual design reflects neatness, and the end product should be easy on the eyes and immediately give an impression of orderliness which will go a long way to impress the reader. Chapter Seven gives two examples of complete CVs laid out in a simple but effective manner.

Although final recruitment decisions are not made on visual presentation alone, as opposed to content, the way information is assembled makes an important first impression and could mean the difference between someone bothering to spend time with your CV or deciding to move on to the next one.

Make sure also when you are typing the information that you use all of the features of the Word Processor (assuming that you are using a WP). Make sure that you have clean margins and that you are consistent when presenting your information. For example, you might want to ensure that your work is not right hand justified as this lends a certain uniformity to a CV. Maybe it is better to leave it unjustified or "ragged right" as it is known.

Quality

Obviously the quality of a CV depends very much on the way it is laid out and the information contained within it. However, it is also true to say that a much better impression is made with a quality paper. There are different qualities and thicknesses of paper and I would recommend that a thicker more durable paper be used, such as Conqueror.

A good quality paper at the outset enhances the effort that you will make when laying out information and presenting yourself in the best light.

Style

By style, I am referring to the way you present information about yourself. Remember that there are two important rules underlying any form of presentation of information, particularly when you have limited space. Be brief and be clear! You do not want to bore the reader by going on and on, using twenty words when five will do. However, conversely, you do not want to be too brief and exclude the main emphasis of what you wish to get across.

Writing the ideal CV is a skilled business and requires thought and concentration, along with creative editing. If possible, I would advise showing the finished product to someone skilled in the art of report writing before you send it to a prospective employer.

As we progress through the book there will be examples of the kind of style you should be aiming for. These examples will build up into a complete CV which should set the standard you are trying to achieve.

The basic structure

Although the basic structure of a CV is well known, it is more important to structure the CV in a way which shows you in the best light.

The traditional structure of a CV is as follows:

Name

Address

Occupation

Telephone number

22

Date of birth

Place of birth

Marital status

Next of kin

Health

Driving license

Religion (if applicable)

National insurance number

(sometimes religion, nationality and passport number
if applying for a job abroad)

Secondary education

Higher education

Professional qualifications

Employment history

Other (interests, achievements etc.)

There are several variants on this approach. Remember, what you are doing is delivering information to the potential employer. This person might well be interested in your employment history at the outset and it may be more effective to deliver this information right at the beginning. Leave the matter of details such as date of birth and secondary education until the end and begin with the most important first.

Therefore, instead of adopting the traditional approach you might want to use the following format:

Name

Address

Telephone number

Career

Achievements

Professional qualifications

Education

Interests

Other personal details

Date of birth

We have considered the most important aspects of the ideal CV. These are quality, style and layout. Finally, there is the content. These initial pointers should enable you to begin to put together your first CV. In the following chapter we will look at the presentation of your personal details and how to obtain the ideal structure.

It is important to remember that I will be following the traditional format when presenting each area of information. It will be up to yourself to rearrange the format as you think best.

Now please read the **KEY POINTS** from Chapter Two overleaf.

KEY POINTS FROM CHAPTER TWO

DESIGNING THE IDEAL CV

- **Your CV should always present a well rounded, balanced picture of yourself**

- **Your CV highlights your potential value to an employer. It should be concise and easy to read**

- **Your CV should be well laid out. Visual presentation is of the utmost importance**

- **Use good quality paper when producing your CV**

- **Be brief and clear when outlining the various areas of your CV**

- **Use a tried and tested format. There are several variations outlined in this book**

Now turn to Chapter Three.

3

PRESENTATION OF PERSONAL DETAILS

As I stated in Chapter Two, personal details do not necessarily come first in your CV but the arrangements of this section are similar in all CVs. The only differences relate to the amount of information given and where it appears.

The most obvious information you should open with is that of your name and address and telephone number. You should also put your occupation.

Date of birth and place of birth

If the CV is being assembled for a single job application then the applicant's age should appear alongside the date of birth. This reduces the reading time of the CV. When the CV is to be used over a long period then the date of birth should be inserted because the passage of time will lead to inaccuracy. The entry giving details about ages of children can also become outdated and therefore it is important to supply date of birth here too.

In addition to date of birth, place of birth should be entered too.

Nationality

Depending on what post you are applying for, and where in the world, you should refer to nationality. If the job is in the United Kingdom, this is not strictly necessary.

Religion

Again, you should only make reference to religion if it is relevant. For most job applications, it is not necessary. For jobs abroad where it is deemed to be of importance you should state your religion.

Marital status

Make reference to whether you are married or single. It is not really necessary to allude to the fact that you are seperated or divorced.

Next of kin

Next of kin should be entered as a matter of course, particularly if the nature and type of work is dangerous.

Passport number

You should make reference to this if the post is abroad. Otherwise it is not necessary.

Health

Another sub heading which may not be used in all instances is that of health. This will apply if physical fitness is an important consideration, jobs such as swimming instructor, physical fitness trainer etc.

Driving license

Details concerning your driving license can be important. A potential employer may be impressed by a clean license. If the license is not clean then you should indicate that you have a full license only.

Relocation

If you wish it to be known that you would be prepared to relocate to another part of the country then you should indicate this. You may not want to be specific here, therefore leaving open the question of relocation.

National insurance number

Your national insurance number should always be included in your personal details. This is particularly relevant when the CV is being used to apply for a job offshore. You should know your own field of work and when to include this information.

Personal details should be presented as in the example below. You may not require all of the information outlined. However, it is important to remember that you are tailoring your details to the potential employer. Obviously, some of the details will be wholly dependent on your prospective employer.

PERSONAL DETAILS

Full Name:	John Smith
Occupation:	Computer Scientist
Address:	38 Cromwell Drive London E17
Telephone Number:	123 6789
Date of Birth:	25 5 52
Place of Birth:	Quality Street Northampton
Nationality:	British
Religion:	Christian
Marital Status:	Married with Daughter aged 4

Next of Kin: Mrs Smith address as above

National ins no: 123456789

Driving License: Current full

Passport Number: 456789

Health: Excellent

Preferred location: Anywhere at all

The personal details section of the CV is straightforward. The most important point to remember is that apart from the obvious information, such as name and address there are important areas which are directly relevant to the job for which you are applying and which you must include.

Now please read the **KEY POINTS** from Chapter Three overleaf.

KEY POINTS FROM CHAPTER THREE

PRESENTATION OF PERSONAL DETAILS

- **Your personal details may vary according to the post offered**

- **If your CV is being assembled for a single job application, mention your age. For multiple applications mention your date of birth**

- **Don't forget to include your name and address. Many people do!**

Now turn to Chapter Four.

4

Presentation Of Education, Qualifications And Training

Obviously, education, qualifications and training will differ according to individual experience. Normally, in a CV you would include education from the age of eleven onwards. It is not necessary to include schools attended prior to secondary schools. Sometimes a person will have attended more than one secondary school, for a variety of reasons, such as parents moving job, and in this case you should normally only include the last two schools.

Your achievements at school, in the form of GCSE (or GCE) should be clearly demonstrated. You might wish to emphasise the most relevant passes first although it is usual to rank the passes in descending order. In addition, you may want to explain your qualifications if you feel that they may not be readily understood because of changes in the school system, i.e., GCEs becoming GCSEs.

Example

JULY 1968

GCSE

English	Grade	(d)
Biology		(c)
French		(c)
Physics		(c)
Economics		(a)

And so on.

Higher Education

For those who have received an education after leaving secondary school, whether it be university or technical college, it is usual to present the nature and type of education and your qualifications. For those who left school and went straight into employment with no formal qualifications it is usual to proceed with your career history.

If you have gone on to higher education then the next stage of the CV will look something like this:

September 1970 - July 1973   Waldesley Polytechnic

High Street Waldesley

Subject   BA Computer Sciences

Grade   2.1

If your further education has been more technically oriented, i.e., part time day release, then the entry would look more like this:

September 1970 - September 1973   City and Guilds

Subject   Computer Science Part 1

Grade   Pass

September 1973 - September 1974   City and Guilds

Subject   Computer Science Part 2

Grade   Pass with merit

The above is only an example and does not relate to the actual Computing syllabus.

It could be that you have attained a number of qualifications during your time at university or college and that you have a long list of diplomas or certificates.

The question to consider here is whether or not to include them all or whether to stick to the relevant ones.

The employer would first and foremost be interested in the qualification which is most relevant to the job being applied for. Then the focus would be on the relevant areas of practical experience underpinning the paper qualification.

Although you may have obtained numerous certificates or diplomas in other subjects, which may well be an indication of intelligence, self discipline and determination, it is really the most relevant qualification which is the most important. The key point to remember is that information overload may serve as a distraction and draw the potential employer's attention away from the most important qualification.

Placements during training

Placements with other organisations, such as industrial placements or college placements, whatever the length should be treated as a normal job in the career history, with the placement clearly emphasised:

Example

October 1973 - April 1974	Finetronics Ltd Long Road Waldesley
Computer Trainee on placement	Assisting the Chief Engineer developing computer systems

Short courses

Over the years an applicant will have attended many short courses either connected with his employment or voluntarily. You should only really make reference to short courses if they have relevance to the job being applied for. Again it is no use entering a proliferation of courses attended if all you are achieving is information overload.

Example

Authentic Electronics Ltd

July (1989)	Fault finding on Computers (2 days)
September (1989)	Software Analysis
December (1989)	Advanced Spreadsheets

Sometimes recruitment agencies will rely on key words when retrieving potential candidates from databases. For example, Comp for computer specialists. If your CV is going to a particular agency it is a good idea to ensure that you are aware of the need to insert any relevant abbreviations which might be used as key words.

Professional Associations

It is at this point, at the end of your formal qualifications and before your career history, that you would insert your professional qualifications, if any. Professional qualifications, in most cases, are obtained following a specialist course and then after a period in the relevant job. A professional qualification is intended to demonstrate that you have received the appropriate amount of academic and practical training and that you are a competent person able to operate in your given field. Therefore, the entry might look like this:

PROFESSIONAL ASSOCIATION:

Royal Institution of Computer Technicians

Date entered: October 1978

If you think it is relevant, you might consider using the letters relating to your profession alongside your name when entering your personal details. The same consideration might also be given to Educational qualifications, i.e., BA (hons).

Service in the Armed Forces

If you have served in the Armed Forces then your education within the military will be emphasised in exactly the same way as the previous example. The potential employer will see at a glance that you were in the forces and will expect to see this in your career history.

Education, Training and Qualifications

Building up on what we have included so far, this section of your CV should look as follows:

Education: 1963 - 1968

Northampton Grammar School

GCE Passes:

English   Grade (d)

Biology   (c)

French   (c)

Physics   (b)

Economics   (b)

HIGHER EDUCATION

1970 - 1973   Waldesley Polytechnic, High Street,
                Waldesley Northampton

BA   Computer Sciences: Pass with distinction

Year One: Computer Theory

Year Two: Advanced Computer Theory

"   "   Computer Trainee on placement,
                ElectronicsSystems Ltd,
                Long Road, Northampton.
                Assisting the Chief Engineer
                developing computer systems

Year Three: Applied Computing

SHORT COURSES

Authentic Electronics Limited

July 1989   Fault finding on Computers (2 days)

September 1991   Software Analysis (1 week)

December 1995   Advanced Spreadsheets
                       (1 week)

PROFESSIONAL ASSOCIATION

Royal Institute of Computers

Fellow of the Institute October 1978

Now you should read the **KEY POINTS** from Chapter Four overleaf.

KEY POINTS FROM CHAPTER FOUR

PRESENTATION OF EDUCATION,
QUALIFICATIONS AND TRAINING

- **Include only education from the age of eleven onwards (secondary)**

- **Your achievements at school should be clearly demonstrated**

- **Rank passes in descending order**

- **Highlight higher education. Emphasise your most relevant qualifications**

- **Emphasise relevant short courses**

- **Be aware of the need to insert relevant abbreviations when sending your CV to recruitment agencies**

- **Highlight professional associations to which you belong**

- **Highlight service in the Armed Forces**

Now turn to Chapter Five.

5

PRESENTATION OF YOUR CAREER HISTORY

So far we have looked at personal details and your education and qualifications. However, it is true to say that it is the next part of your CV which will be of the most interest to the would be employer.

This section, of all sections, will demand the greatest amount of time and thought as employers will be looking to see what sort of experience you can bring to their organisation. Although your education may be first class and your qualifications second to none they will almost always take second place to your actual experience in a particular field.

When producing this area of the CV (as with all areas) avoid long flowing prose and avoid the use of the first person, i.e., I\we, as your document will only usually get a quick first reading and therefore lots of irrelevant information may put off the potential employer. Familiarity in a CV will usually go down very badly indeed so stick to the facts and be objective.

You should always begin with your current employer first (or most recent) devoting the most time and space here as it is the one the potential employer will see as most relevant. The standard procedure is to catalogue your jobs in reverse order, showing the name and business of the employer, the dates of employment in months and years and the job and duties.

The material must be well organised in this section to enable the employer to see where your main strengths are. The exact address of the organisation is not needed but is helpful to indicate the area. Some people do not name their company. This is not recommended. It gives the impression that they are ashamed of it and makes it harder for the person assessing the application to get a feel for what the individual was doing.

Many things are deduced by the reader, taking into account the job title, the company business and size and the list of your duties. These things all contribute to helping to build up a picture of the sort of work undertaken and leaving out the company name denies the reader some of that information.

You will not need to give details of the grades of your previous positions. This would be irrelevant to a new employer and in any case the recruiter is unlikely to know the details of the grading structure of your last employers. Although you may have been in a high grade, omit details of this. Ensure instead that you put in information on any promotions that you gained. You may also want to mention merit increases gained, although this may be done through the covering letter rather than the curriculum vitae.

In cases where you have undertaken a number of similar jobs, amalgamate these into one section if this is feasible. Give a brief outline of the duties with the caveat that you had similar employment in those companies and give inclusive dates.

You do not have to include reasons for leaving, or salary. However, you might want to indicate the salary for your current/ last employment in order to give the prospective employer an indication of what salary you might be asking for.

Your career history

Taking into account the above, the section of your CV dealing with your career history would look as follows:

CAREER HISTORY

April 1989 - current.

Authentic Computers, Northampton. Consultant

In this post, I am acting in the capacity of consultant to the private and public sectors, advising on systems usage. I am employing the technical know how gained in my previous jobs.

I am conversant with most computer packages

Salary: £25,000 Per Annum

February 1984 - March 1989

London Borough of Shepwhich. Senior Computer Manager

In this post, I had responsibility for overseeing a change in the authority's computer system. This involved carrying out systems analysis and producing a brief for the council, who subsequently accepted the brief and instructed the computer department to effect the change.

After two years I was promoted from Computer Manager to Senior Computer Manager.

February 1983 - February 1984

I took one year out from work to fulfil ambition to travel around the world with my wife.

May 1975 - January 1983

Wing Computers Limited, North Circular Road, Northampton

Whilst employed by Wing I obtained the status of Fellow of the Royal Institute of Computer Scientists. My main duties for the company were to oversee the development of a computer system for a local authority. This involved giving technical advice to the authority and supervising a workforce of 23 people who were directly involved in the installation of the equipment.

During this time, I gained experience of the following packages:

Wing 1 - Wing 2 - Super Wing-Wing for Windows

April 1974 - May 1975

Barnard Computers Limited, Northampton

Whilst in this post, I commenced my professional Institute Exams. My main duties were to assist the Deputy Chief Executive in developing a new operations system.

Now read the **KEY POINTS** from Chapter Five.

KEY POINTS FROM CHAPTER FIVE

PRESENTATION OF CAREER DETAILS

- This section of your CV is the most important area of the document

- Avoid long flowing prose. Avoid the use of the person

- Begin with your current employer first, listing jobs in reverse order

- You do not have to include details of salary, with the possible exception of current or last employer

- You do not have to include reasons for leaving. However, you may wish to make reference to this separately, depending on the reason

Now turn to Chapter Six.

6

OTHER INFORMATION

In addition to the main points of your CV, you may feel that it is necessary to include other details. The following covers main areas of further information which may assist the interviewer in the initial stages of the job hunting process.

Health

Unless you have had a serious illness which you feel that the potential employer should be aware of, then it might be wise to omit this. The person scrutinising your application will assume that you are in good health unless you state otherwise.

If you have spent time away from employment due to illness, and there is a gap in your CV then it might be wise to explain this separately, emphasising that there are no recurring problems and that you are fit for work.

One point worth remembering is that employers with over 20 employees are required by law (1944 Disabled Persons Employment Act) to employ a quota of three percent of disabled persons in the workplace. The Act only deals with registered disabled and is very difficult to enforce, however.

References

Omit references unless you are specifically asked for them. Where you are asked to give references, use your most recent or current employer if possible and the one immediately prior to that. If you are applying for your first job, be prepared to use a tutor at your school or college.

Whenever you give the name of referees, ask the individuals first if they are willing to provide a reference for you.

Salary

This is another detail which can generally be omitted, especially if your employment history spans a number of years.

Payments received several decades ago are not relevant now. The employer is more interested in your most recent salary, as they will, more often than not, base their decision on this information.

If your salary is good in your current post, you may want to leave details of this out as it may deter a would be employer who may be offering a low salary. If your current salary is poor, the reader may wish to know why that is the case. Therefore, you may wish to leave this blank too.

Hobbies (interests)

You should think carefully about what you will include here. Try to tailor it to the post you are applying for. Try to list interests which show a balance. A healthy interest in sport and the outdoors should be counterbalanced by other, more intellectual pursuits.

In general, keep this section short as it is an extra which you are adding in order to give the reader a more complete picture of you.

Languages

You should make reference to languages that you can speak, other than your mother tongue, only if they are pertinent to the post applied for. Only give information about languages that you can speak if you really know them. It is no good embellishing the truth and being shown up at an interview.

Other

Make reference to your driving license. Usually, employers like to see that you have a license, although with some jobs it is not relevant. If you have produced any publications that might be relevant to the post, make reference to these. Generally, it is the more academically inclined jobs which feel publications are relevant. However, other employers offering legal or advice posts might be suitably impressed if you have produced work which has been published.

Experience in the Armed Forces usually impresses employers as it denotes a person who has been subject to a life of organised discipline and would probably turn out to be a trustworthy employee. This, of course, may not always be the case but general perceptions are most important when getting beyond the first stage.

Now you should refer to the two examples of complete CVs in **Chapter Seven.**

7

EXAMPLES OF COMPLETE CVS

The following are examples of two different layout styles of a CV. The information is the same and includes all elements. However, you should include, and exclude, information depending on the perceived requirements of the employer. For example, it may not be necessary to include religion or location or other facts. This depends entirely on the employer.

Example 1

PERSONAL DETAILS

Full Name:	John Smith
Occupation:	Senior Computer Manager
Address:	38 Cromwell Drive London E17 8HN

Telephone Number:	0181 123 6789
Date of Birth:	25 5 55
Place of Birth:	Northampton
Nationality:	British (only enter if necessary)
Religion:	Christian (only enter if necessary)
Marital Status:	Married with one daughter aged 5
Next of Kin:	Mrs Smith, address as above
N.I. Number:	123456789
Driving License:	Current full
Passport Number:	345678 (only if necessary)
Health:	Excellent
Preferred Location:	Anywhere (only if necessary)

EDUCATION, QUALIFICATIONS AND TRAINING

1963 - 1968

Northampton Grammar School

GCE Passes:

English	Grade	**(d)**
Biology		**(c)**
French		**(c)**
Physics		**(b)**
Economics		**(b)**

HIGHER EDUCATION

1970 - 1973

Waldesley Polytechnic, High Street, Waldesley
Northampton

BA Computer Sciences:	Pass with distinction
Year One:	Computer Theory

Year Two: Advanced Computer Theory

" " Computer Trainee on placement, Electronic Systems Limited, Long Road, Northampton. Assisting the Chief Engineer developing Computer Systems

Year Three: Applied Computing

SHORT COURSES

Authentic Electronics Limited

December 1990 Fault finding on computers (2 days)

September 1991 Software analysis (1 week)

December 1995 Advanced Spreadsheets
(1 week)

PROFESSIONAL ASSOCIATION

Royal Institute of Computer Scientists

Fellow of the Institute 1990

CAREER HISTORY

April 1989 - Current.   Authentic Computers. Consultant.

In this post, I am acting in the capacity of consultant to the private and public sectors. My most recent job was to advise Tenby Local Authority on the renewal of their computer system.

I am thoroughly conversant with all computer packages and have travelled abroad in my capacity of consultant advising international companies.

Salary: £25,000 Per Annum

February 1984 - March 1989.   London Borough of Shepwhich. Senior Computer Manager.

In this post, I had responsibility for overseeing a change in the authority's computer system. This involved carrying out systems analysis and producing a brief for the council, who subsequently accepted the brief and instructed the computer department to effect the change.

I was promoted from Computer Manager to Senior Computer Manager after two years.

February 1983 - February 1984. Travelling.

During this period, I took the opportunity to travel the world with my wife, before settling down with my family.

May 1975 - July 1983. Wing Computers, North Circular Road, Northampton

Whilst employed by Wing, I obtained fellow status in the Royal Institute of Computer Scientists. My main duties for the company were to oversee the development of a computer system for a local authority. This involved giving technical advice to the authority and supervising a workforce of 23 people who were directly involved in the installation of equipment.

During this time, I gained experience of the following packages:

Wing 1 - Wing 2 - Super Wing-Wing for windows.

July 1974 - May 1975. Barnard Computers Limited, Nottingham

Whilst in this post, I commenced my Professional Institute Exams. My main duties were to assist the Deputy Chief Executive in developing a new operations system.

PERSONAL INTERESTS

I am interested in squash, badminton and indoor football. In addition, I am interested in studying history, particularly the history of computing science from the 1930's. I enjoy walking in the countryside and swimming. I also like to participate in the community and am on the local conservation committee.

I speak French and German fluently and have travelled to these countries for my current employer on business.

HEALTH

Excellent

PREFERRED LOCATION

London

Example 2

Name:	John Smith
Address:	38 Cromwell Road London E17 8HN
Telephone Number:	0181 123 6789
Occupation:	Computer Scientist

CAREER

April 1989 - Current. Authentic Computers Limited, Consultant

In this post, I am acting in the capacity of consultant to the private and public sectors. My most recent job was to advise Tenby Local Authority on the renewal of their computer system.

I am thoroughly conversant with all computer packages and have travelled abroad in my capacity of consultant advising international companies.

Salary: £25,000 Per Annum

February 1984 - March 1989 - London Borough of Shepwhich, Senior Computer Manager

In this post, I had the responsibility for overseeing a change in the authorities computer system.

This involved carrying out systems analysis and producing a brief for the council, who subsequently accepted this and instructed the department to go ahead.

I was promoted from Computer Manager to Senior Computer Manager after two years.

May 1983 - February 1984 - Travelling

During this period, I took the opportunity to travel the world with my wife before settling down with my family.

May 1974 - July 1983 - Wing Computers, Northampton, Computer Manager

Whilst employed by Wing, I obtained fellow status in the Royal Institute of Computer Scientists. My main duties for the company were to oversee the development of a computer system for a local authority and to supervise a workforce of 23 people who were involved in the installation of equipment.

During this time, I gained experience of the following packages:

Wing 1 - Wing for Windows - Super Wing-Wing 2

July 1974 - May 1975. Barnard Computers, Northampton. Computer Trainee.

Whilst in this post, I commenced my professional examinations. My main duties were to assist the Deputy Chief Executive in developing a new system.

PROFESSIONAL QUALIFICATIONS

Fellow of the Royal Institute of Computer Scientists, 1990

EDUCATION

1963 - 1968

Northampton Grammar School

GCE Passes:

English	Grade	(d)
Biology		(c)
French		(c)
Physics		(b)
Economics		(b)

HIGHER EDUCATION

1970 - 1973

Waldesley Polytechnic, High Street, Waldesley, Northampton.

BA Computer Sciences: Pass with distinction

Year One: Computer Theory

Year Two: Advanced Computer Theory

Year Two: Computer Trainee on placement, Electronics Systems Ltd, Long Road, Northampton. Assisting the Chief Engineer developing computer systems.

Year Three: Applied Computing

SHORT COURSES

Authentic Electronics Ltd

July 1989	Fault finding on Computers (2 days)
September 1991	Software Analysis (1 week)
December 1995	Advanced Spreadsheets (1 week)

INTERESTS

I am interested in squash, badminton and indoor football. In addition, I am interested in studying history, particularly the history of computing science after the 1930 s. I enjoy walking in the countryside and swimming and like to participate in the community and am on the local conservation committee.

I speak fluent French and German and have travelled to these countries for my current employer, on business.

OTHER PERSONAL DETAILS

Date of Birth:	25 5 54
Place of Birth:	Northampton
Marital Status:	Married with one daughter aged 4
Next of Kin:	Mrs Smith, same address
N.I. Number:	123456789
Driving License:	Current full
Health:	Excellent
Preferred Location:	Anywhere

The above two examples represent two different ways of laying out your CV. The information is the same but presented in a different way. The reader will see different facts first, You must decide what will be of primary importance for this particular employer.

The key point is that you are presenting what you consider to be the most important and relevant facts first. Example one concentrated on personal details first, followed by education then career. Example two placed immediate emphasis on career then education, with personal details last.

The first example is the traditional way of laying out a CV. However, you must give thought to which elements you wish to present first in order to make an immediate impact.

Now turn to **Chapter Eight.**

8

PARTICULAR CVs

School leavers

Most school leavers will have very little experience of the job market, with the exception of a Saturday job, or evening employment. The fact that you do not have a career history to demonstrate should enable you to keep this part of your CV brief. Generally, you should aim to keep to one side of A4 paper.

Your education will be the most important part of your CV if you are a school leaver. You should try to include any work experience you may have had. This will include work experience programmes and Youth Training programmes.

Generally speaking, you should list all work experience. Highlight grades achieved. However, if they are not good overall, omit them. The employer can ask for details if these are needed. You will invariably have to explain the nature of the qualifications. If you are

67

older then the school system will have changed. However, if you are about to leave school then the would be employer may not understand your qualifications.

One example is that employers are now getting used to the grading systems of the GCSE and GNVQs (General National Vocational Qualifications) and would possibly be out of touch or not see the relevance of GCE "O" levels.

You should attempt to make a connection between your hobbies and your personal qualities which show your skills and aptitudes. Organisational skills are generally valued and participation in voluntary work can help to create a positive image of you as a person.

Do try to avoid quoting too many interests or giving the impression of a "flighty" person, in that you flit from one hobby to another. The employer is usually more concerned that you are able to settle into a work environment, especially as you have not experienced the world of work and the attendant discipline required.

If you have been involved in the arena of student politics, be careful how you mention this. Some employers are not overkeen to employ someone who they perceive may cause disruption or upset a well established applecart. There is no harm mentioning areas of responsibility such as president of your branch of the National Union of Students, but don't go much beyond this, unless of course you are known to a prospective employer and your political skills and history are an asset.

Long term unemployed

If you have never been employed, or if it has been many years since you were in employment, the main problem that you will encounter is explaining the gap in your employment and demonstrating that you are still employable. At all costs you must avoid giving the prospective employer the impression that you feel hard done by or have a chip on your shoulder. Employers want to take on cheerful employees, not those disgruntled and harbouring past resentments. At the end of the day, you have a selling job to do and it will be no easy task to convince an employer that you are ready to re-enter the world of work.

Redundancy

If you have been made redundant, try to show that you understand the company's reasons behind the re-organisation or whatever. If the organisation went out of business, show that your attitude towards this was responsible and do not let the reader of the curriculum vitae think that this was in any way due to you.

Show that you have somehow learned from the experience by doing something positive which will help you in your future career. If you have undertaken formal training to prepare for a career change or advancement, be specific in how that training fitted the job applied for in the new company.

If you are circulating many unsolicited applications, you must still tailor these to the organisations and the kind of jobs that you are interested in there. Your application is wasted without this. In unsolicited applications ask if they have any current vacancies for the sort of post you are seeking, or whether their future planning indicates that any may be available in the near future. Remember to include your most positive points, including the ability to work immediately. This can be a very valuable plus point in your application.

Career breaks

If you have had a career break to raise a family, for example, or are changing career direction it can be very difficult to convince a prospective employer that you are serious about the post and are committed to it. You must convince the employer that you are now firmly committed to working and that you have a real interest in their field of work. Cite any refresher courses that you may have taken and emphasise that your child care arrangements are adequate.

Your career change may be due to circumstances beyond your control. If you have undertaken retraining, sound positive about this and indicate that it was thorough and you took it seriously.

If you are returning to work after a spell in prison, note the Rehabilitation of Offenders Act 1974. This covers people with certain past convictions but who have not been convicted again for specific lengths of time. After these trouble free periods, the individuals are deemed to have "spent" their convictions and do not have to declare them.

If the conviction has no bearing on your prospective employment and you can avoid mentioning it, do so. However, you must not lie about it and may have to declare it if asked.

If you are returning to employment in the United Kingdom after working abroad, you must show how the position you held abroad was similar to the kind of job you had here. The recruiter must be convinced that the change in culture would not mean that your training and abilities have a completely different slant. You may be able to stress the positive side of this too, emphasising your increased awareness of the international business scene.

If you have worked overseas, references may be difficult for the employer to follow up. Testimonials, translated as necessary, may be useful in this situation.

Now please read the **KEY POINTS** from Chapter Eight overleaf.

KEY POINTS FROM CHAPTER EIGHT

PARTICULAR CVs

- If you are a school leaver, keep your CV brief and to the point

- Your education will be the most important part of the CV

- Include any work experience you may have had, however brief

- Make a connection between your hobbies and personal qualities. Try to avoid quoting too many interests

- If you are long term unemployed, be positive and avoid giving the impression that you are disgruntled or are resentful

- If you have been made redundant, try to portray your redundancy in a positive light. If you have undertaken formal training since being made redundant, be specific in how that training fits the job applied for

- If you have had a career break, you must convince the prospective employer that you are now fully committed to returning to work

Now turn to Chapter Nine.

9

THE IDEAL COVERING LETTER

A covering letter with your CV is really a letter of introduction and is usually the first thing that a prospective employer reads. You should always send a covering letter with a CV or application form. If your application is speculative, this is even more important.

The reason for sending the letter is to make sure that the prospective employer has all the facts. Make sure that you keep a copy of what you send.

Rules of letter writing

Ensure that you use a good quality paper, ideally A4 so that it fits well with other documentation, do not use coloured paper with elaborate designs. Most employers cannot stand this approach.

Your letter can be typed or handwritten as long as the end result is that it is legible. If a person cannot read your letter then they will dispose of it, along with your

CV. If you know that your handwriting is bad, then type the letter.

Use black ink for writing or typing letters as this makes it easier for photocopying. The usual rules of spelling and grammar apply in letters as they do in the CV. The overall effect has to convince the reader that they are dealing with a professional.

Any letter that you send must be formal. It must be well set out and show respect to the person that you are writing to. Remember, if you start the letter by saying "dear sir" you must end by saying "yours faithfully" and that if you use the person's name then you must end with "yours sincerely". Note that the "f" and "s" are in the lower case.

Note how the title of the recipient is given in the advertisement. If the text asks you to reply to a specific person then you should do just that. Always address the person by their surname and never their forename.

Put your address in the top right hand corner of the letter. You should not put your own name here but leave it until the end of the letter, where you will print and sign. You can, if necessary, put your telephone number underneath your address.

If you put the name and address of the recipient, this should be further down the page on the left hand side. Depending on your style of letter, the date can either be beneath your own address or under the recipient's address.

Space the letter out as well as you can. Again, the main rule of letter writing is that the recipient has to get a clear impression of the writer. The more legible the letter, the better laid out, the better the impression. If the letter is short, such as a letter requesting an application form then you should start further down the page.

If there is lots of information in the letter, then you should commence higher up the page. If you can possibly fit all on one side then all the better.

Below, you will see an example of a letter forwarding a CV to a prospective employer. Following this, you will see a further two examples. The first one is requesting an application form. The second is returning an application form to a prospective employer.

Example 1

38 Cromwell Road
Walthamstow
London E17 9JN

Tel: 0181 123 5678

Daniel Green
Raft Enterprises
Codley Way
Northampton
N1 F45

6th May 1996

Dear Mr Green

Your Ref: ABCDEFG. Computer Scientist

I would like to apply for the position of Computer Scientist with your company. I saw the advertisement in the Times newspaper on Friday, 3rd of May 1996.

As you will see from my enclosed CV, I have been a Computer Manager since I graduated from Northampton Polytechnic in 1973. I have been involved in the public and private sectors, overseeing systems analysis and installation.

I believe that I have the experience you are seeking and would be very interested in working for Raft Enterprises.

I look forward to hearing from you.

Yours sincerely

John Reynolds

Example 2

38 Cromwell Road
Walthamstow
London E17 9JN

Tel: 0181 234 5678

Mr J Baldrick
Baldrick Enterprises
Jones Street
Northampton
N1 4RG

6th May 1996

Dear Mr Baldrick

Your Ref: COMP 123. Computer Manager

I am responding to your advertisement in the Times newspaper for a Computer Scientist. Could you please forward me an application form.

I look forward to hearing from you.

Yours sincerely

John Reynolds

Example 3

38 Cromwell Road
Walthamstow
London E17 9JN

Tel: 0181 234 5678

Mr J Baldrick
Baldrick Enterprises
Jones Street
Northampton
N1 4RG

8th May 1996

Dear Mr Baldrick

Please find enclosed my application form for the post of Computer Manager advertised recently in the Times newspaper.

I look forward to hearing from you soon.

Yours sincerely

John Reynolds

Letters to agencies/consultants

Again, when writing to agencies and consultants, employ exactly the same rules of letter writing but be more specific about what you want if you are writing general letters, not in response to a specific advertisement.

You may wish to give the consultant more information so that he/she can suggest vacancies that you may be interested in applying for. You need to convince the consultant that you are proficient in your chosen field. Therefore, your application must look professional. Remember that it will go from the consultant to a number of companies.

The golden rule throughout letter writing is that a letter must be laid out on quality paper, well written, clear and to the point.

Now you should read the **KEY POINTS** from Chapter Nine overleaf.

KEY POINTS FROM CHAPTER NINE

THE IDEAL COVERING LETTER

- **Always send a covering letter with a CV or application form**

- **Use good quality paper**

- **Type your letter if your handwriting is bad**

- **Use black ink**

- **Letters must always be formal**

- **Spend time laying out your letter. Double check it when you finish**

- **Be brief and be clear!**

Now turn to Chapter Ten.

10

APPLICATION FORMS

If you are applying for a job which requires you to fill an application form in, there are several rules to remember. When you receive the form, never fill in the original in the first instance. You might make a mistake or not be happy with what you have written and want to start again. Too late!

Always copy the form and fill it in with a pencil. This way, you will not suffer if you make a mistake.

Application forms can either be hand written or typed. It is up to you to exercise your discretion at this point. However, only if your handwriting is neat should you fill in the form by hand. A typewritten form will be more immediately readable and make a better first impression.

Send the application form in with a brief covering letter. Do not falsify the application form, as this will form part of your contract of employment when offered the post.

The job application should be treated much the same way as your CV. As we discussed, when you interpret the job advertisement, you need to analyse the nature of the job before compiling your CV.   You should do exactly the same with an application form.The first task is to read the job description which should normally accompany the application form.   It is absolutely essential that you understand the requirements of the post.

Many organisations will send a person specification with the application form. the person specification outlines the essential and desirable criteria which the applicant must meet before he or she is considered for the post.

Although the essential criteria are the most important, if those shortlisting for the post have a number of good candidates then they will revert to the desirable criteria as a way of further eliminating candidates.

It follows that, when you are completing an application form which has a person specification in it, then you should fill in the application carefully following the requirements of the post, ensuring that you meet the essential and desirable criteria.

In addition to essential and desirable criteria, there will normally be a skills required section which will generally outline the skills and abilities which the person must demonstrate.

Make sure that when you fill in your application form that you follow the person specification closely, you have read and understood the job description and that you comply with all the requirements. If you do not then you are wasting your time.

Normally, there is a space on an application form which asks you to outline your experience to date and to demonstrate why you want the job. You should be concise and to the point here.

On too many application forms, applicants really go to town in this section, producing a whole life history amounting to many sides of paper. This is totally unnecessary and will, more often than not, end up with your application form being thrown in the bin.

You should follow carefully the requirements of the post , from the job description and person specification and lay out clearly and concisely your experience to date. You should then relate this to the post on offer and explain why you think you are the ideal candidate.

If there is no job description or person specification to work from, then you will need to read very carefully the requirements of the post from the advertisement and then construct what you think are the main aspects of the job related to your own experience. In this way you can present the interviewer with a picture of yourself. It is not very often nowadays that an application form is not accompanied by a job description.

If you feel that you are on uncertain ground, for example when faced with filling in an application form without a job description or person specification, then you might want to contact the company concerned and request further information.

Content of application forms

The application form will proceed on a logical progressive basis, much as a CV is compiled. The form will start by asking you your name and address. Some will ask you your date of birth. The type of organisation you are applying to will very much determine the application you are being asked to fill in.

Some application forms are designed with great care and reflect the ethos of the organisation, such as omitting to ask certain information on an equal opportunities ground. For example, some organisations deliberately do not ask for details concerning age as this is thought to affect the perceptions of those who are shortlisting for the post.

There will be a space for a phone number. This is very important as the company may want to contact you by phone shortly after an interview to discuss the possibilities of offering you a job.

Other details at the beginning of an application form might be sex, marital status and country and place of birth. This again will vary depending on the organisation you are applying to.

The next section of the form will ask you for your educational details. Here, you should start with your most recent job first. However, it is important to read the application form as it might state otherwise.

Application forms might ask for salary information and reasons for leaving the post. As we discussed, on a CV it is not wise to volunteer this information, with the exception of final salary. However, some application forms may require this and will say so.

If the state of your health has not involved disability, but has involved long periods off work then you should try to demonstrate to your employer that this problem is now in the past and that this will not affect your future employment.

Most applications will finish by asking for references. These will usually be your current employer and sometimes a previous employer or someone who can give you a character reference. Make sure that you know what the employer is going to say about you in advance. It follows that you should let that person know that you are going to use them as a reference.

Many employers do not take up references despite asking for them. Others always take them up as a matter of course. Some application forms state that they will take up references when a candidate is shortlisted. You should contact the company and state that you do not want this as it could affect your relationship with your employer (if this is the case).

If you have not yet been employed, then you should use school or academic references. A second reference might be a personal reference. Some applications will ask specifically for a personal reference. In this case, it is better to use a professional reference, i.e., someone with whom you may have worked in a voluntary capacity or even someone for whom you have done paid work.

There are a number of other questions which may appear on an application form, such as whether or not you have a driving license or whether you speak any other languages. Notice periods, possible start dates, membership of professional bodies and details of when you can attend an interview may also appear too. There may also be a requirement to outline your ambitions. Be careful and tailor this to your employer's requirements.

Now you should read the **KEY POINTS** from Chapter Ten overleaf.

KEY POINTS FROM CHAPTER TEN

APPLICATION FORMS

* **Always fill in a copy of the original application form. Use a pencil to do it. Only when you are happy with the end product should you transfer it to the original.**

* **Type the form unless your handwriting is very neat.**

* **Send the form with a brief covering letter**

* **Read the job description and person specification carefully. Fill the form in following the requirements of the post**

* **Be concise and keep to the point, particularly in the "experience to date" section of the form**

* **If there is no job description or person specification and you are in doubt, then you should contact the company concerned and request more details**

* **Check with potential referees before using them**

Now go to Chapter Eleven.

11

OFFERS OF EMPLOYMENT (OR OTHERWISE)

How you conduct an interview is beyond the scope of this book. Suffice to say that you need to be well prepared and confident (not over confident) and fairly assertive.

Answer the questions put to you clearly and concisely. Be direct and if you get stuck don't try to bluff your way out of it. Be honest and direct and either ask the interviewer to clarify the question or say that you are not exactly sure of that particular answer and that you would like to come back to it later, or you don't know the answer.

If you don't get the job

If you receive a letter or phone call informing you that you did not get a particular job, then it is wise to request feedback from the interviewer. It is very important indeed to get an idea of where you went wrong. It could be that you performed excellently, but someone else just pipped you to the post. Failing to get a job can lead to feelings of rejection and can undermine your confidence, particularly if you have had a number of interviews.

The main reason for getting feedback is that you could be making the same mistake over and over again without knowing it. Maybe you get aggressive in an interview situation and start to attack the interviewer. Maybe you dry up because you feel intimidated. Whatever the reason, you require continuous feedback to enable you to fine tune your interview technique.

In addition to this, several organisations exist which will help you to improve your interview skills, often free of charge.

Offers of employment

If you are offered a post, you should wait until you receive the offer in writing before making your next move. The offer letter should contain everything at the interview.

Some letters offering employment are formal and give you all the information that you need to know. Others are not so clear and you need to clarify certain details. You should write back immediately on receiving an offer of employment. You should not keep the employer waiting because you think that you may be offered a job elsewhere.

There are several things that you must confirm before accepting a job:

- Starting salary
- The grade of your job within the company structure
- Probationary periods
- Notice periods
- The arrangements for salary reviews
- Whether the offer is subject to satisfactory references
- Details of company car arrangements if applicable
- Promotion prospects

The exact details of the contract of employment including holidays, pension, hours of work etc.

You may not need to check all of the above, but the important thing to remember is that you should detail all the things important to you and ensure that they are clear before commencing employment.

You must clarify your exact salary before you start, as this can cause misunderstandings and mistrust at a later date, if there were only vague promises at the outset, such as "we will see what we can do later".

Now read the **KEY POINTS** from Chapter Eleven.

KEY POINTS FROM CHAPTER ELEVEN

OFFERS OF EMPLOYMENT (OR OTHERWISE)

- **When you attend the job interview, be smart, be confident and reasonably assertive**

- **Answer questions clearly and concisely**

- **If you do not get the job, you should request feedback about your performance**

- **If you do get a job, make sure that all the important points are clarified before accepting**

Now turn to the final points.

FINAL POINTS

Putting together your CV takes time and effort. It is a job that many people put off until the last moment. However, by doing this you quite often end up rushing the final job.

As you have seen on your journey through this book, a lot of information needs to go into a CV. However, more importantly, the relevant information, well laid out on quality paper, concise and to the point will almost certainly make an immediate impression on the reader.

You need to pay particular attention to the job advertisement. All too often, a CV is completed which bears no relation to the actual post on offer. This is because the writer of the CV has gone off on a tangent. Read the job description carefully, along with the person specification if there is one. If necessary, contact the company concerned requesting more details.

Follow the simple principles of layout as demonstrated in this book. Don't send irrelevant details. The examples in this book included all information. However, you may want to include or exclude information depending on the job.

When you get to the interview stage, remember: be relaxed and confident and answer questions carefully, sticking to the point.

If you fail to get a job, request feedback. If you get a job, make sure that the terms and conditions are clear and in writing.

The best of luck with your job hunting!

OTHER STRAIGHTFORWARD GUIDES
IN THIS SERIES

A Straightforward Guide to:

The Rights of the Private Tenant
Computing
Divorce and the Law
Teaching Your Child to Swim
Small Claims in the County Court
Personal Finance
Teaching Your Child to Read and Write
Accounts and Book Keeping for Small Business
Leaseholder's Rights
The Straightforward Business Plan
Tiling for Beginners
Setting up Your Own Business
Car Mechanics for Beginners
Caring for a Disabled Child
A Voter's Guide to the General Election

For a catalogue of existing and forthcoming publications, contact:

Straightforward Publishing
38 Cromwell Road
Walthamstow
London E17 9JN
Tel: 0181 521 6168